EDGE BOOKS™

The Real World of Pirates

PIRATE GEAR

CANNONS, SWORDS, AND THE JOLLY ROGER

By Liam O'Donnell

Consultant:
Sarah Knott, Director
Pirate Soul Museum
Key West, Florida

Capstone
press®

Mankato, Minnesota

Edge Books are published by Capstone Press,
151 Good Counsel Drive, P.O. Box 669, Mankato, Minnesota 56002.
www.capstonepress.com

Library of Congress Cataloging-in-Publication Data
O'Donnell, Liam, 1970–
    Pirate gear : cannons, swords, and the Jolly Roger / by Liam O'Donnell.
    p. cm.—(Edge Books. The real world of pirates)
    Summary: "Presents the tools and equipment pirates used for daily life at
sea, as well as the weapons used for their deadly raids on merchant ships"—
Provided by publisher.
    Includes bibliographical references and index.
    ISBN-13: 978-0-7368-6425-1 (hardcover)
    ISBN-10: 0-7368-6425-3 (hardcover)
    1. Pirates—Juvenile literature. I. Title. II. Series: Edge Books, the real world
of pirates.
G535.O364 2007
910.4'5—dc22   2006001003

Editorial Credits
Aaron Sautter, editor; Thomas Emery, designer; Jason Knudson, illustrator; Kim Brown,
    production artist; Wanda Winch and Charlene Deyle, photo researchers

Photo Credits
Art Resource, NY/Erich Lessing, 14 (bottom); HIP, 27
Capstone Press Archives, 13 (bottom)
Corbis/Bettmann, 8–9, 10–11
Courtesy of the Pirate Soul Museum, 9 (bottom), 14 (top), 15, 18 (top)
The Granger Collection, New York, 23
Mary Evans Picture Library, 24
North Wind Picture Archives, 18–19 (bottom), 26
Peter Newark's American Pictures, 4
Peter Newark's Historical Pictures, 7, 19, 21, 22, 28–29
Peter Newark's Pictures, 9 (top)
Rick Reeves, 16–17
SuperStock, 12; Superstock/age fotostock, 13 (top)

1 2 3 4 5 6 11 10 09 08 07 06

TABLE OF CONTENTS

CHAPTERS

FEATURES

Chapter One

TOOLS OF THE TRADE

Pirates were fierce fighters when raiding a ship. Along with gold, they often stole guns, food, and other supplies.

On a warm July night in 1720, Captain Samuel Cary saw strange ships sailing close. Black flags flew from their masts. The flags were painted with a man and a skeleton toasting a drink. The ships belonged to Bartholomew Roberts, also known as Black Bart. Roberts was a cruel pirate who had raided many ships and stolen much treasure.

But Roberts wasn't looking for treasure on this raid. Instead, the pirates took guns, sails, ropes, and food. Black Bart's crew needed something more important than treasure—they needed pirate gear.

Sea Smarts

Pirates sailed the oceans stealing from other ships. For many pirates, it was the only job they knew. Like other workers, pirates needed the right tools for the job.

Learn About:
- Navy sailors
- Keelhauling
- What pirates stole

One of a pirate's best tools was his knowledge of the sea. Pirates were some of the best sailors in the world. Many pirates had first been sailors in the navy. The navy taught them how to find their way using only the sun and the stars as guides. Many sailors left the navy because of low wages or cruel captains. Some chose to use their sea knowledge to become pirates. They wanted to live a life of adventure while searching for treasure.

EDGE FACT

Cruel navy captains punished disobedient sailors with keelhauling. The man was tied with a rope and pulled under the ship. Victims' bodies were slashed by razor-sharp barnacles, and most were drowned. Many sailors left the navy and turned to piracy just to escape this deadly punishment.

Experienced pirates kept their ships on the right course even in bad weather.

Pirates desperate for supplies often dared to raid larger, better-armed ships than their own.

Tool Robbers

Pirates needed tools other than their sailing skills to sail their ships. Ropes, sails, and pistols were all important gear.

When pirates needed gear, they couldn't buy it at the nearest harbor. Because they were criminals, pirates risked being thrown in jail if they were caught. To get new sails, food, or clothing, pirates attacked ships and stole the things they needed.

When raiding ships, pistols and axes were favorite pirate tools.

Chapter Two

SETTING SAIL

Sailing a ship was hard work. Pirates had many jobs to do. The crew worked together as a team. They used many kinds of gear to keep their ship sailing smoothly.

Strong Sails

Sails were like engines for a pirate ship. Sails caught the wind and helped push the ship through the water. Sails were made from a sturdy canvas called sailcloth.

Learn About:
- Types of sails
- Ropes and knots
- Navigational tools

Like other sailors of long ago, pirates relied on their ship's sails to speed across the oceans.

Sails came in many shapes and sizes. Each type of sail was named for its place on the ship. The large mainsail hung from the mainmast in the center of the ship. Spritsails hung from the long bowsprit that stuck out from the front of the ship. The more sails a ship had, the faster it could sail. Some ships had ten or more types of sails.

Large square mainsails caught lots of wind, allowing ships to sail quickly across the ocean.

Pulley Power

Pirates had to adjust the sails to keep the ship moving quickly and safely. They used ropes and pulleys to raise and lower the sails. This block and tackle made moving the heavy sails easier.

Pirates also used many ropes called rigging to help them control the sails. To hang the sails and secure the rigging, pirates had to know how to tie many kinds of knots.

Knot Know-How

Knots served many different jobs. A short splice tied two pieces of rope together. The spritsail sheet knot tied down the spritsail at the front of a ship. To untie knots, pirates used a sharp iron spike called a marlinspike.

A = Masthead knot
B = Short splice
C = Sheep shank with sword knot

A

B

C

13

Charts and Spyglasses

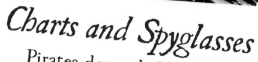

Pirates depended on their sailing knowledge and ocean charts to find their way. Charts showed pirates where dangerous rocks, shallow water, or safe harbors were located.

The navigator read the charts and kept the ship on course. He used a spyglass to spot land on the horizon. This small telescope helped him track the ship's location on the chart.

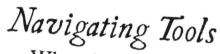

Navigating Tools

When the navigator couldn't see land, he used an astrolabe and compass to keep the ship on course. Astrolabes measured the position of the sun or the stars in the sky. Navigators compared their readings with journals to figure out where their ship was on the ocean chart. Navigators used compasses to see what direction the ship was sailing.

Ocean charts were valuable treasures. In 1682, Bartholomew Sharp stole ocean charts from a Spanish ship. When he was caught by the British navy, the charts were so useful that the king gave Sharp a full pardon and called him a hero.

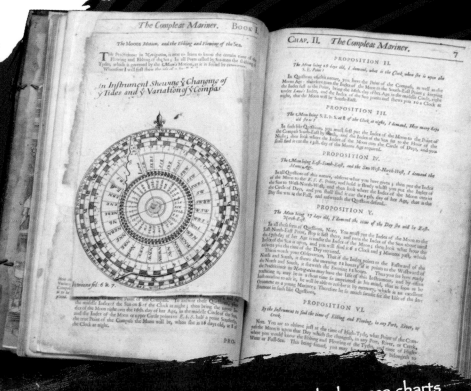

To keep their ships on course, pirates relied on sea charts and navigational journals. Journals described things like the direction of ocean currents and the positions of stars.

Chapter Three
READY FOR BATTLE

Pirates were always hunting for treasure, but they weren't willing to die for it. Unless they were desperate for supplies, pirates only fought battles they could easily win. If a merchant ship looked too strong, they left it alone. But when pirates did get into battles, they had the right gear to raid a ship and capture the treasure.

Stink Bombs

Sometimes, pirates smashed clay jars filled with burning sulfur and rotten fish guts onto the decks of merchant ships. The pirates hoped these stink bombs would make the merchant ship's crew too sick to fight.

Learn About:
- Battle techniques
- Guns and blades
- The Jolly Roger

Grappling Hooks

Pirates also used grappling hooks to attack merchant ships. The sharp spikes of these hooks dug into the deck of a merchant ship. The pirates then pulled on ropes tied to the hooks to bring the two ships close together. Pirates could then easily jump on board the ship they had just captured.

Cannonballs

Cannons were the most powerful of all pirate weapons. These heavy guns fired many types of ammunition. Pirates usually loaded them with cannonballs. These heavy metal balls crashed into wooden ships, smashing everything in their path. Pirates also used small metal balls called grape shot in cannons. Grape shot caused damage over a wide area. It shattered ship hulls, and easily ripped through both sails and men.

With weapons like grappling hooks and deadly cannons, pirates were feared by many merchant ship crews.

Swords and Pistols

When pirates boarded merchant ships, a bloody battle was underway. Short swords called cutlasses were deadly in a crowded fight. Many pirates also carried a short knife called a dagger. It was designed for stabbing. These blades made pirates deadly in close combat.

Edward Teach, better known as Blackbeard, carried up to six pistols into battle.

Pirates also fought with guns. The flintlock pistol was a favorite pirate weapon. It was easy to aim and small enough to carry in one hand. Because the flintlock pistol only held one shot, some pirates carried several of these loaded guns into battle.

EDGE FACT

Pirate flags were called Jolly Rogers. Early pirate flags were all red. The French called them *jolie rouge*, which means "pretty red" in English. Some people think the term Jolly Roger came from this French name. Some famous pirate flags are shown below.

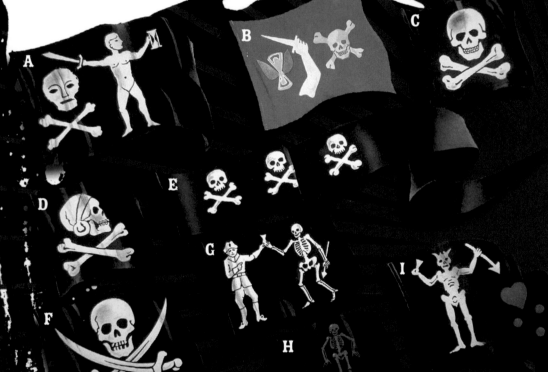

A = Walter Kennedy; B = Christopher Moody; C = Edward England; D = Henry Every; E = Christopher Condent; F = "Calico Jack" Rackham; G = "Black Bart" Roberts; H = Edward Low; I = Blackbeard (Edward Teach)

Pirate Flags and Reputation

One of the most useful pirate weapons didn't sink ships or kill people. It was the pirate flag, and it struck fear into the hearts of merchant sailors. Skeletons, daggers, bleeding hearts, and other frightening images were painted onto these red or black flags. Each pirate had his own flag design.

Every sailor had heard stories about the cruelty of pirates. These stories gave pirates a deadly reputation. When merchant captains saw a pirate flag, they often let the pirates board their ships without a fight. They preferred to give up their treasure easily, rather than be tortured or killed.

Chapter Four

PIRATE SURVIVAL KIT

Some pirates buried treasure on remote islands. But most pirates usually only stopped at islands to restock their water and food supplies.

Battles for treasure weren't the only dangers pirates faced. Their ships were cramped, dirty, and often filled with deadly diseases. Boredom could also be a problem on long voyages. To avoid these problems, pirates had special gear to keep them healthy and entertained.

Fresh Water

One of the biggest challenges of life at sea is finding enough fresh water to drink. In the 1700s, all ships carried large barrels filled with fresh drinking water. When they ran out, pirates landed on remote tropical islands to fill their water barrels from rivers and springs.

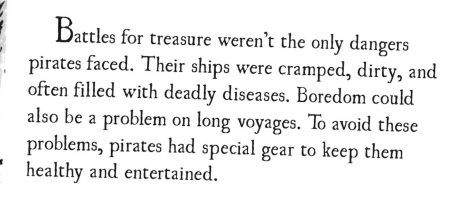

Learn About:
- Fresh water and grog
- Pirate entertainment
- Losing a limb

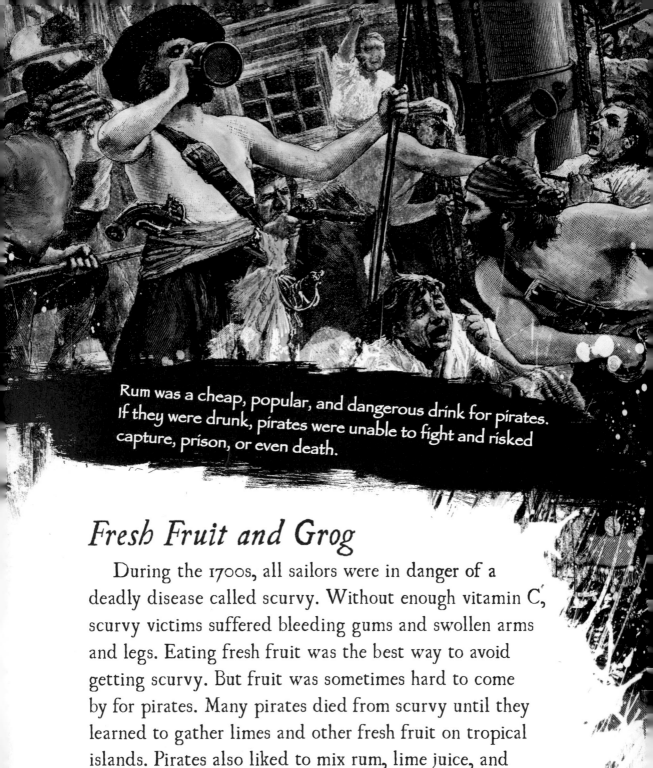

Rum was a cheap, popular, and dangerous drink for pirates. If they were drunk, pirates were unable to fight and risked capture, prison, or even death.

Fresh Fruit and Grog

During the 1700s, all sailors were in danger of a deadly disease called scurvy. Without enough vitamin C, scurvy victims suffered bleeding gums and swollen arms and legs. Eating fresh fruit was the best way to avoid getting scurvy. But fruit was sometimes hard to come by for pirates. Many pirates died from scurvy until they learned to gather limes and other fresh fruit on tropical islands. Pirates also liked to mix rum, lime juice, and water to make a favorite drink called grog.

Cards, Dice, and Parrots

Between raids on merchant ships, pirates often became bored at sea. They played games with cards or dice to help pass the time. But playing for money was forbidden on many ships. Gambling often led to deadly fights between pirates.

Pirates often captured parrots or monkeys to sell in Europe or America. But some pirates kept these animals as pets. Some historians believe the image of a parrot perched on a pirate's shoulder came from their practice of keeping pets.

Pirates always kept their weapons clean and ready to fight. They never knew when they might find a merchant ship loaded with treasure and new gear.

Strike Up the Pirate Band

Some pirate ships had their own band. The band played songs to entertain the pirates. During a pirate raid, the band played fearsome war music on trumpets and drums. The loud noises scared the merchant ship's crew and encouraged the pirates to fight harder.

Studying Pirate Gear

Charts, weapons, and sails were essential pirate tools. Pirates relied on their gear to fight, steal treasure, and sail across the ocean. Today, historians study many of the items pirates left behind. From spyglasses to cutlasses, museums hold many of the things that made pirates the most feared sailors on the sea.

EDGE FACT

Most pirate ships didn't have doctors. If pirates were badly injured in battle, they went to the ship's cook to cut off injured arms or legs. Few pirates survived this crude surgery. Those who did often used a hook or a peg leg in place of the missing limb.

Glossary

ammunition (am-yuh-NISH-uhn)—bullets and other objects that can be fired from weapons

astrolabe (ASS-truh-layb)—a tool used by a ship navigator in the early 1700s to measure the position of the sun and stars

bowsprit (BOU-sprit)—a long pole that extends from the front of a ship and holds the front sails

cutlass (KUHT-luhs)—a short sword with a curved blade

mainmast (MAYN-mast)—a tall, strong pole in the center of a ship that holds the ship's main sails

rigging (RIHG-ing)—the ropes on a ship that support and control the sails

scurvy (SKUR-vee)—a deadly disease caused by lack of vitamin C; scurvy produces swollen limbs, bleeding gums, and weakness.

spyglass (SPYE-glass)—a small telescope that makes faraway objects appear larger and closer

Read More

Platt, Richard. *Pirate*. DK Eyewitness Books. New York: DK Publishing, 2004.

Steer, Dugald. *Pirateology: The Pirate Hunter's Companion*. Ologies. Cambridge, Mass.: Candlewick Press, 2006.

Williams, Brian. *Pirates*. A First Look at History. Milwaukee: Gareth Stevens, 2005.

Internet Sites

FactHound offers a safe, fun way to find Internet sites related to this book. All of the sites on FactHound have been researched by our staff.

Here's how:

1. Visit *www.facthound.com*

2. Choose your grade level.

3. Type in this book ID **0736864253** for age-appropriate sites. You may also browse subjects by clicking on letters, or by clicking on pictures and words.

4. Click on the **Fetch It** button.

FactHound will fetch the best sites for you!

Index